THE INVISIBLE ELEPHANT –
Exploring Cultural Awareness

Tom Verghese
The Cultural Synergist

Published by Synergistic Press

Synergistic Press
Level 5, Causeway House
306 Little Collins Street
Melbourne VIC 3000
Australia

Email: info@culturalsynergies.com

First published 2006

Second edition 2007

National Library of Australia
Cataloguing-in-publication entry

Tom Verghese
The Invisible Elephant – Exploring Cultural Awareness
ISBN 0-9775967-0-2

1. Cultural diversity   2. Cultural awareness   3. Working across cultures

Printed in Australia
Edited by Leon Krason
Designed by Ideazz & Koncepts

For further information contact Synergistic Press on
+61 3 9654 6161 or email: info@culturalsynergies.com

DEDICATION

This book is dedicated to my parents Thomas and Sosamma who provided all their four children with the experience of developing intercultural competence by encouraging and modelling it themselves.

– Tom Verghese

ACKNOWLEDGEMENTS

This book is a result of the efforts and synergies of a number of people.

My thanks to the project team: Lisa Taliga, my Virtual PA; Leon Krason, my editor, for organising the material; Natalie Trott, my proofreader; Chaun Soh, who designed and managed the publication; and Mike Street, my sounding board.

My clients, for enabling me to expand my knowledge and learn by working with their culturally diverse teams. They include among others: Shell, BP, Autoliv, University of Melbourne, ANZ Bank and AchieveGlobal.

My many friends, whose ideas and dialogue sharpened my thinking, especially Dr. Mark Brophy, Duncan Smith, Graeme Smith, Dr. Ed Trost, Vince Amato, Fiona Hyde, Dr. Asma Abdullah, Dr. Alan Weiss, Jayne Robertson, and Dr. Palan.

My siblings, and their spouses, scattered around the globe: Joe and Diana, George and Shanta, and Anu and Arnold. Our family gatherings are always an intercultural event.

And for their love and total support: My wife, Alison, and children, Jemma and Rajesh.

— Tom Verghese

ENDORSEMENTS

What people had to say about the first edition of *The Invisible Elephant*:

"*The Invisible Elephant* reads like a global Melway (Melbourne's street directory), mapping major roots to cultural intelligence... Naming the sites we each need to experience as global citizens and businesses.

Since reading *The Invisible Elephant* I am less self critical and nervous about doing the right thing, knowing that I now have compass points with which to navigate cultural difference".

Catherine van Wilgenburg
Director
Living Colour Studio

"The material in this book will enhance learning and future generations. It should be essential reading for all principals, teachers and students".

Michael Giulieri
Principal
Essendon North Primary School
Melbourne

"It's great... A quick read, well organised. It explained why some things I know work do work, and gave me some new insights".

Ian Chalmers
Director
Training and Sales Systems
Ingersoll Rand Industrial Technologies
Asia Pacific

"With just a few hours of reading, I got many important insights of cultures impact on all kinds of results".

Ulf Sjodin
HR Director, Region Europe
Leadership Development
Autoliv Development AB

"This book blends deep understanding of the subject with an ability to engage the reader... It is easy to absorb, but never simplistic. An exceptional leadership tool for any organisation working trans-nationally or with a multi-cultural workforce".

Jill Lever
Head of People Capital
Esanda

"Working across cultures is a critical skill for all global managers... The Cultural Mirror is a useful tool to help understand differences and similarities".

Woon, Lai Har
Senior Shell Learning and Diversity Consultant
Shell Eastern Petroleum (Pte) Ltd.
Singapore

"Highly recommended. After reading the book, I was able to engage the untapped ideas and energy in my team... and they delivered extra-ordinary performance".

Sharann Johnson
HSSE Manager, IST-EH
BP Singapore

"*The Invisible Elephant* is an excellent guide to helping anyone venture the unavoidable maze of crossing cultures. Absolutely relevant in this day and age of globalisation!".

Suma George
General Manager
OnCard Private Ltd, Singapore

"This book is a vital contribution to the cause of cultural understanding and to creating an environment of synergistic unity in the workplace. Practising what you learn in this book, will assists you in accelerating towards success in gaining the competitive business advantage!"

Linda Banks
Human Resources, Organisational Development and Training
Portland General Electric Company
USA

"Very easy read, concise and straight to the point. Recommended reading for anyone serious in succeeding in a diverse environment".

Sim Chee Kian
BP Singapore

"An invaluable resource for each and every one of us to better understand and appreciate all cultures, including our own, and how to use that knowledge to enhance our day to day interactions and activities".

Robert Main
Manager, Equity and Social Justice
Victoria University

"Tom Verghese takes the reader on an insightful journey through the 'cross-cultural maze' and provides wonderful 'Aha' moments for those working with people with different cultures. It is easy to read and hard to put down".

Jane Toone
Senior Consultant, People Capital & Change
ANZ Bank

"I recommend *The Invisible Elephant* for those struggling with the challenges of leading across culture, time and distance… This new book will further assist with developing the capabilities of leaders at all levels of organisations".

Cheryl Woollard
General Manager
Global Human Resources
Air International

"Working in the health industry, this book provides a simple reminder of how culture impacts on us all …where communication is so vital and health professionals have been taught within a Western framework this is essential preliminary reading for all."

Jane Howard
Nursing Team Leader
Western Health

"A logical book to recommend to anyone dealing globally or with diverse cultures – it highlights the need to do a little "thinking" first before we do anything with people. Thanks once again for a great book."

Ruth Maitland
Managing Director
Maitland Consulting Group

"Having travelled across many different countries and worked with different people from varied backgrounds and cultures, I could fully identify with contents of the book.

An excellent fact highlighted in your book is that we must first be aware of our own cultural programming – this is key, self discovery and awareness is the first step in the journey to be able to understand others that are different from ourselves."

Sara Allen
Director – APAC
Sara Lee Information Centre of Excellence

"*The Invisible Elephant* made my perspective of my national culture in comparison to my personal culture more visible. It has given me a deep insight into dealing with people of different cultural backgrounds."

Asma Ghabshi
Learning and Development Manager
Shell Oman

CONTENTS

PREFACE

This book is based on workshops that I have facilitated around the world for my global clients. A repeated request from participants has always been for an easy to read, informal book that they can dip into on a regular basis. Learning about culture is an ongoing developmental process. We can never know all there is to know about the many different cultures on this planet. Each culture is unique, but for brevity I am generalising about cultures in this book.

I hope you find the concept of the 'invisible elephant' useful in helping you increase your awareness and knowledge about culture. Culture influences everything we do – often subconsciously. I have attempted to make this book user-friendly and non-academic. There are references at the back for those of you interested in wanting to know more.

The structure of the book is in three main parts. The first part is focused on defining culture and why you should pay attention to it. The second part describes a framework that you can use to understand cultural differences and similarities. Examples are provided from a number of different countries. The third part is about developing strategies when dealing with people from different cultures.

I hope you enjoy the book and that it stimulates your thinking.

CHAPTER 1

GLOBALISATION AND CULTURAL AWARENESS:
THE ELEPHANT ENTERS THE ROOM

"All people are the same. It's only their habits that are so different."
Confucius

Globalisation is happening and it isn't going to stop. Every business is now potentially global. There are 6.5 billion people on this planet and many of them are moving, due to business, war, natural disaster or economic opportunity.

Some of them will work with you, study with you and even move into your neighbourhood. Most people today work, live and play in a community populated by people from diverse religious, cultural and belief systems. Keep in mind that we share many commonalities, but also many differences. Each of us was raised in a specific country and culture, with its own traditions and belief systems.

You can embrace these changes, hate them or feel anything in between. The reality of the world today is if you can't adjust to them positively, you will be disadvantaged.

Dealing with these issues, which are cross-cultural, is rather like dealing with an elephant in your lounge room. One you can't see. You know it's there, as you have to deal with the results. Unless you learn to live in harmony with it, the elephant can destroy your surroundings. Cross-cultural issues need to be treated in the same way. Ignore them and they may cause issues.

Even when we know the problems we are having are related to these cultural issues, we often pretend they are not there – hoping they will go away. They won't.

You have taken an important step in dealing with the elephant – simply by starting to read this book.

Its purpose is to improve your understanding of all cultures, including your own. By introducing a number of models and frameworks, this book will enhance Cultural Intelligence. Cultural Quotient (**CQ**) or Cultural Intelligence is having the knowledge, the skills and the attitudes to interact effectively with people of different cultural backgrounds.

If you are working in the average company today, you already know the importance of interacting effectively with people of different cultures. Whatever your role in the world today, it will be impossible to fulfil it tomorrow without some degree of cultural awareness.

An improved **CQ** will result in an awareness and capacity to build a more inclusive workplace by celebrating cultural diversity and enhancing future directions.

The next chapter will explore why this is important.

CHAPTER 2

CONTROLLING THE ELEPHANT:
THE USE OF CULTURAL SYNERGIES

"The world learns slowly, but ultimately it learns, or rather it
unlearns old dogmas."
Handy, 2002

We live in a new world order. New businesses are born every day. Every
business relies on its team making it profitable. Synergy is created when a
group of individuals blend into a great team. What then is synergy?

Taken from the Greek word "sunergos", it means that a group
of individuals working together as one unit can produce better results
than any individual member. According to Buckminster Fuller, synergy
involves, "…a new way of thinking…which helps to free one from
outdated patterns and can break the shell of permitted ignorance" (Adler,
1997). It is a dynamic process involving constant adaptation, reappraisal,
learning, and integration.

It does not signify compromise. No one gives up anything
– everyone gains something.

A number of models will be presented further in this book
demonstrating various processes to achieve synergy. Cultural synergy
builds upon the very differences in culture for mutual growth and
accomplishment by cooperation. Through collaboration, it emphasises
similarities and common concerns and integrates differences to enrich
human activities and systems.

We must leap at the opportunity to learn from our differences
and leverage that learning for competitive advantage, rather than hide,
ridicule or ignore them.

Unless we use all the skills and wisdom that every culture holds,
how can we move forward? Those who embrace the available knowledge in

the post-modern world will pass you by. Doing this is not the responsibility of world leaders, corporate leaders or anthropologists. It is the work of all of us – every individual. In this time of cross-cultural organisations, communities and even families, it is more vital and important than ever before.

The elephant shares our space. We work together with it so that each understands the other's requirements. Its trunk vacuums our room and sniffs out trouble. We give it succour and comfort. We, and the elephant, both gain. There is no loss. Only wins. The companies whose individuals grab the elephant by the trunk are those who will reap the rewards in the post-modern world.

We cannot start to develop cultural synergies without first understanding culture. And we cannot appreciate cultural differences without initially being aware of our own, and that is what follows in the next chapter.

CHAPTER 3

CULTURE: HOW THE ELEPHANT WAS BORN

"Years of study have convinced me that the real job is not to understand
foreign culture but to understand our own."
Hall, 1959

The global, political and business challenges of the new century will be
more about culture than about technical or industrial issues. Culture
must be managed carefully just like any other business policy or process.

In most Western languages, the meaning of the word 'culture' is
comparable to 'civilisation', or 'refinement of the mind' and the results of
such refinement, for example: education, art and literature. This definition
of culture is narrow and meaningless in the post-modern globalised world.

Gert Hofstede, a Dutch anthropologist, defines culture as "a
collective programming of the mind which distinguishes the members
of one category of people from another". So – it's a mental state and it's
about groups of people.

Culture is the context through which we construct our world
– the window that filters our view. I like to think of it as the 'lens' through
which we look out to the world. Be it familial, natural, religious, social,
ethnic, corporate, racial or linguistic, culture is **learned**, not inherited.

- attitudes
- judgements
- values
- belief systems
- morals
- needs, wants and desires
- identities
- opinions about who **'we'** are

AND EVEN MORE IMPORTANTLY
- who **'they'** are.

In other words, culture defines our reality. Culture is so entrenched in us that we don't notice it. We do not see it. As the invisible elephant sits in our room, so culture sits invisibly in our minds, our hearts and our subconscious.

Culture is also shared within each group. It is a collective phenomenon, and enables us to communicate easily with fellow members of our group. It includes the most mundane things in life:

- how we greet each other when we meet
- how and when we eat
- how we dress
- whether we are demonstrative or show few feelings in emotional situations
- how we maintain our bodies and our hygiene
- our marriage customs
- when and how we work
- our religious ceremonies
- our leisure pursuits.

We always use our own culture as a standard of measurement, usually judging our culture as normal and good, and that, which is different, as abnormal, bad and not as refined and developed as ours.

Our culture becomes self-referential, and this is bound to create incorrect perceptions and misunderstandings because no other culture is identical to our own.

Each society has a certain set of problems in common with other societies. For example, the problem of caring for dependent members such as the very young and the very old. The solutions to these common problems are culturally determined, and therefore, they vary from society to society. Solutions provided by one society may be regarded as indefensible by those in another.

Consider this extreme example. Under certain circumstances, 'geronticide' (the killing of elderly people within a certain society or population) has been practised for centuries by some nomadic Eskimos and Caribou Indians. If the old and infirm are too feeble to keep up with the group, they are, by necessity, left behind to die. The practise of geronticide is a culturally defined behaviour pattern, designed to ensure the survival of the group in times of extreme food shortages and hardship. Like many of the customs of non-western societies, this practice appears strange and heartless to some westerners, but in the context of that particular society, it is sensible, rational, and an accepted way of life.

We must avoid thinking of culture as a 'thing' in isolation that exists on its own and that may cause or create an action. It is through social interaction and evolution that a culture moulds a people. A culture does not actually 'do' anything. It can be observed in the regular and typical behaviour of a people or group. It is therefore vital to understand that there is **no** 'normal' or **'right'** culture. There is just 'culture' or a way of being.

To each culture there are actions which are right and normal, and others are judged on how well they 'fit in' to the prevailing culture.

These are, however, commonalities in all cultures. In 1954, Albert Maslow developed a hierarchy of needs – common to all humans. They range in importance from bottom up. As each need is met, we rise up the hierarchy of needs. See the following diagram.

Maslow's hierarchy of needs

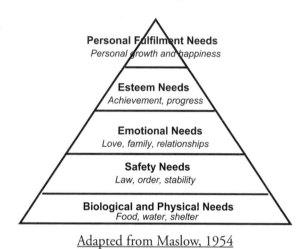

Adapted from Maslow, 1954

Even within the commonalities, culture does create differences. For example, we may all want to laugh and enjoy life. However, the things that make us laugh tend to vary from culture to culture.

Consider British humour versus American humour, or any other country you may choose as an example. We may find the intricacies of humour overwhelming, but there are definite distinctions in the wording, inflection, delivery and physicality of humour from one country to another. We may all love to laugh, but what we find funny is culturally bound.

As stated earlier, national, or country culture, is defined by the beliefs, rituals, norms, values and behaviour practised by and embraced by the people of a particular nation. At its simplest, consider the cultural norm of bowing in Japan, the importance of a handshake in Australia or the kiss on the cheek and the hug that is so prevalent in Italy.

Organisational and corporate culture

The culture in an organisation or company is specific to the way the organisation has evolved, its practices, policies and politics. Without conscious effort, every employee of a company begins to comply with the company culture as soon as he or she is hired.

It does not take long for a new employee to know how and when to speak up and express an opinion, whether to formally or casually communicate among the levels of management in the organisation, whether it is appropriate to discuss one's personal life with co-workers, and whether honesty is the best policy when talking to a boss or subordinate.

Consider the automobile industry. How different do you think the company culture might be for Toyota as compared to BMW or Chrysler? Although all three are successful car manufacturers, their corporate culture is quite distinct.

Consider that perhaps its Japanese roots influence the Toyota company culture, while Chrysler may be more influenced by its American roots and BMW by its German heritage.

Personal culture

This is YOUR culture. While your familial, national, religious, company and other affiliated cultures permeate your very being, the most basic filter you have is your personal culture.

Your personal culture is your belief and value system, your behaviour, your demeanour when you are alone, or with family, friends and co-workers. It is who you REALLY are. It is both learnt and inherited.

If you consider that who you are as a person is a combination of your personal culture, your national culture and your community and/or organisational culture, you can start to truly understand the complexities of cross-cultural communication.

This is represented in the following two diagrams. It illustrates that all of us develop a unique individual culture, but at the same time have a shared culture with others and with a genetic commonality with other human beings on the planet.

Three levels of uniqueness in human mental programming

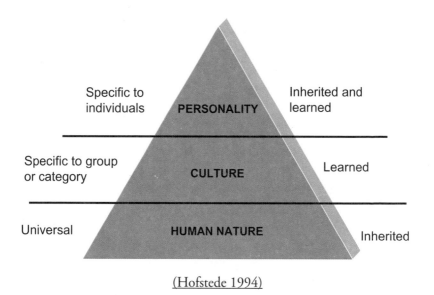

(Hofstede 1994)

If we do not first understand our own perspective and frame of reference, we can never hope to understand the differences and similarities between us and someone else.

Your own culture is subconscious and subjective. It has taken years of subtle conditioning from many sources to form. It is still developing and will continue to develop.

Three culture model

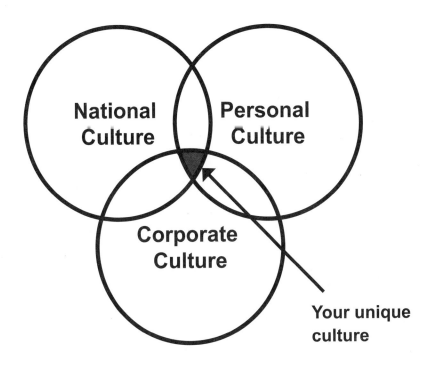

(Gardenswartz, Rowe, Digh & Bennett, 2003)

Now is the time for you to consciously become mindful of the sources of your behaviours. The thoughts that control your actions all have a source. The elephant comes from somewhere. When you have identified the source of your personal culture, you can then take the first steps to understanding another's.

Here is a personal example:

I grew up in Malaysia and my parents are of Indian heritage. As an Indian-Malaysian child, I became accustomed to eating my food with my fingers. A few years before I married my English wife, I took her to visit my family. My wife wanted to demonstrate her cultural sensitivity during this visit and told me that she planned to eat her food with her fingers while she was visiting my family home.

I told her I thought it was a great idea!

Now, picture this scene:

We are gathered around the dining table for our first meal with my parents and siblings. We are eating rice, curry, yoghurt and other traditional specialties.

Five minutes into the meal, my bride-to-be jabs me in the ribs and whispers, "How do you stop the curry and yoghurt from running down your hand?"

I thought about the question for a moment and admitted that I didn't know the answer! The fact is I had never really thought about it. I had eaten this way since I was a child and never *had* to give it a thought.

If you think about this example for a moment, you can probably come up with several of your own. Consider the things that you take for granted as fact or the things you presume everyone knows.

Chinese children can use chopsticks at three or four years of age, yet a European adult using them for the first time has no idea what to do with them.

How we deal with conflict, illness, death, sexual orientation, sexual interaction, sub cultures, interpretations of logic and rationality are all culturally based. Naturally there are always people who do not fit within their own cultures. But most people fit within 90% of the cultural norms of their group, as illustrated in the following diagram.

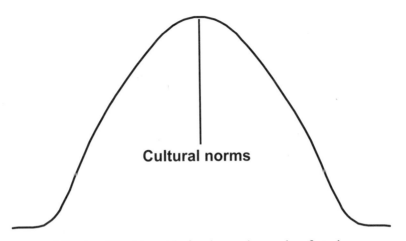

<u>Allowing 5% either side for those who tend to fit in lesss
with their own cultural norms.</u>

You have a unique set of finger prints, and a one-of-a-kind DNA that *only* belong to you, just as you have your own unique perspective and perception.

Culture is a basis. It establishes the foundation from which we make judgments, form opinions and formalise decisions.

Let us focus on the people at the centre of the group, those to whom the norms *do* apply. For them, this group or foundational culture has established a generally accepted way of thinking and behaving, one that is considered 'normal' in their world.

Each family in this culture will teach its children how to fit into their society and culture, and the children will learn the rules of behaviour and protocols appropriate to it.

So, we are usually unaware of other cultures until we travel to another country or visit another place where people live and think differently. We often believe that a major obstacle to world peace or international business is that others **just won't understand the way we think.**

As mentioned earlier, it is vitally important for us to understand our **own** culture and beliefs and consider how they affect our ability to see through the eyes of someone from another culture.

It is a challenge to educate ourselves on our own paradigms and cultural conditioning and to evaluate our own psychological constructs – the way we infer meaning in events, conversations, behaviours and experiences in our lives.

If you want to be enlightened and aware of the impression your cultural traditions and beliefs make on other cultures, ask a foreign national to describe business people from your country.

You should also consider the sayings, slang and proverbs from your country.

Take a moment now to consider some of your sayings and proverbs, and try to imagine what someone from another country might conclude about your country and culture if they heard these sayings or some slang. Reflect on what you find funny and humorous.

Are there subtle inferences that you understand because you were raised in this country? Would everyone understand the meaning of these sayings or might they be misunderstood or misconstrued? Often **negatively**.

If we can see ourselves through the eyes of other people and other cultures, we can modify our behaviour to emphasise our most appropriate actions and effective characteristics and minimise those that are least helpful and may result in misunderstandings.

If we are culturally self-aware, we can predict the effect our behaviour will have on others.

The first step in managing cultural differences is to increase your general cultural awareness, and appreciate the influence your specific cultural background has on your own mindset and behaviour.

While our underlying assumption may be that global leaders should engender change, it is imperative that we realise that these global changes must begin with each individual. It is ever more incumbent on those who wish to interact with others across the globe. Without cultural awareness, any business in the post-modern world will find it difficult to be successful.

By being interested in culture, it becomes possible for us to understand why certain cultural groups behave in the way they do.

Look at the following diagram.

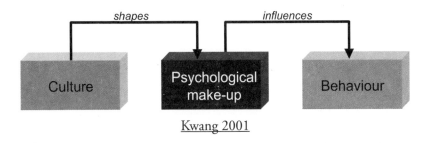

Kwang 2001

This model shows that the particular culture of a society influences and shapes a person's psychological make-up, which in turn shapes and influences their behaviour. For example, in the Japanese culture, the norm is that direct confrontation is to be avoided. Therefore, there is a tendency to maintain social harmony. Compare this with Israel where the norm is to speak up and therefore have a more confrontational, direct style of behaviour.

Is one style better than the other? Am I just stereotyping the two cultures above? Let's look at that in the next chapter.

CHAPTER 4

CULTURAL AWARENESS: RECOGNISING THE ELEPHANT

"That's the way we do things around here."
Anon, 1967

Everybody stereotypes. Even if you think that you don't – think again. You do it without conscious thought. Learned thought patterns dictate the way you see the world. And the way you see others.

Stereotyping involves a form of categorisation that organises our experience and guides our behaviour toward groups. Stereotypes never describe individual behaviour. They are an **outsider's** description of the behavioural norms of a particular group and cause us to attribute characteristics to a person solely on the basis of their membership in that particular group.

Stereotypes are often based on inaccurate preconceptions. In the communication process – especially across cultures – stereotyping can often lead to misleading impressions of others and false conclusions about their motives, actions and goals. The idea that Asians are 'inscrutable' is an example of such a stereotype. It reveals a larger, underlying misconception: that Asia is an amorphous mass, homogenous in the majority of its characteristics. In reality, the Asia Pacific is a region of deep contrasts. While there is a cultural core within Asia (mostly derived from China and India), every country has a unique set of national characteristics. As a result, the label 'Asia' is problematic, blurring fundamental differences within the region. Asia is no more a nation than is Europe.

Our being ethnocentric and parochial usually causes our negative stereotyping of 'others'. **Ethnocentrism** is defined by *Random House Dictionary* as, 'Belief in the inherent superiority of one's own group and culture; it may be accompanied by feelings of contempt for those others who do not belong; it tends to look down upon those considered as foreign; it views and measures alien cultures and groups in one's own culture' (in Harris & Moran 2000).

Ethnocentrism can stifle effective communication across cultures, blocking the exchange of ideas and skills among people. This excludes other points of view and leads to a rejection of the richness and knowledge of other cultures. Avoiding ethnocentrism takes conscious and continuing effort, and requires acceptance of the fact that everything in a particular culture is consistent to that culture and makes sense if you understand that culture.

Parochialism means viewing the world solely through one's own eyes and perspective. A person with a parochial perspective neither recognises other people's different ways of living and working, nor appreciates that such differences have serious consequences.

Stereotyping, ethnocentricity and parochialism are all results of being culturally unaware and insensitive.

A key step in becoming culturally aware is to *accept* that we unconsciously stereotype 'others'. Be aware too that 'others' stereotype us. Question the stereotypes, assumptions and perceptions. We will discuss more of this in Chapter 6.

The word stereotype was first used by journalist, Walter Lippman, in 1922, to describe judgments made about others on the basis of their ethnic group membership (Jandt, 1995). Some examples are, "Australians are easy-going, the French are arrogant, and blacks are dirty". Today the term is used more broadly, to refer to negative or positive judgments made on the basis of any group membership (Jandt, 1995). Anthropologists, Jean-Pierre Gruere and Jean-Pierre Morel, argue that "stereotypes better describe those who formulate them, than those to whom they are directed".

Cultural awareness builds bridges by acknowledging various frames of references and understanding that paradigms *can* and *do* influence how we behave and think.

If we are truly living in a world with a global economy today, and if, as we all acknowledge our families, communities and corporations are a blend and mix of various cultures and values, our challenge is how to leverage these differences to give us a richer, more complete solution or outlook.

How then do we increase our effectiveness when working and living with people around the world? How do we market a product more effectively in China? How can we succeed in an overseas assignment and live comfortably in a foreign country? How can we share and bond with newfound friends and co-workers in their culture and society? Step back from your own assumptions and presences and analyse **your** culture and **the specific cultural experience of another person.** Let's look at that in the next chapter.

CHAPTER 5

THE CULTURAL MIRROR:
NINE DIMENSIONS OF CULTURE

"Let my house not be walled on four sides, let all the windows be open.
Let all the cultures blow in, but let no culture blow me off my feet."
Mahatma Gandhi

Author, Asma Abdullah, created a model, which I have adapted for this book. This model can be used to assess a particular culture, although it does not contain **every** aspect of culture. The model is based on nine dimensions and can assist you as you travel, visit, work and interact with people from different cultures.

I have used this model in many of my workshops around the world, and participants have said they find it useful to reflect on their own cultural background. It is a simple, two-dimensional model, which provides a framework to understand cultural differences and similarities.

The nine dimensions are as follows. Think about your own preferences as you read them.

1. Relationships – Task

In a work situation, do you prefer to spend time getting to know the other party first, or do you like to just get on with the task at hand?

In countries including most of Europe, Asia and the Middle East, the focus is on 'relationships'. It is considered essential to form a relationship before focusing on a specific task. People must feel that they like and trust the other party, at least in a preliminary way, before they can feel comfortable working together. Getting things done in these societies depends on a web of relationships. Therefore, throughout their business lives, people in these cultures cultivate and nourish relationships.

By contrast, in countries such as Sweden, Australia and Canada, people are primarily concerned with the 'task' at hand. For example, Swedes typically approach a project by outlining the overall goal, designating each of the major steps and then addressing staffing needs. Their approach moves from task to people. Indonesians on the other hand, first need to know who will manage the project and who will work on it. Once they know who the leader will be, and the hierarchy of people involved, they can assess the project's feasibility. The Indonesian's approach goes from people to task.

Here is a story that exemplifies the notion of 'building a relationship' to get the tasks done.

I have a Melbourne-based client who is the director of IT for Asia pacific. She's a very highly focused, highly professional individual. Half of her team is based in Manila. In her early days, when she used to go to Manila to visit her team, she would always be taken out to lunch. Lunch in Manila would last for **one and a half hours**. *She was used to having lunch for* **twenty minutes**, *and usually a sandwich at her desk. She couldn't understand why this team wanted to take her out and spend so much time at* **lunch**. *They would also ask her lots of personal questions, such as: how old she was, how much money she made, why she wasn't married – questions she considered to be rather intrusive and personal.*

She evaluated these behaviours to be a waste of time, unprofessional and *lazy*. When she came to be aware of the Philippino culture, she understood that all the team was doing was 'building a relationship'. She decided to change her attitude, make the most of it and catch up with her work later in the day. What she discovered by doing this was that the tasks were completed quicker, more cohesively and she gained higher productivity from her Philippino team, because she used 'relationship building' to get the tasks done.

2. Harmony – Control

What is a person's relationship to the world? Do you believe that you can shape your surroundings and events or do you feel that you must submit to nature's whims? Are people dominant over their environment, in harmony with it, or subjugated by it? This dimension involves people's relationship to the external environment, including *nature*.

Western societies tend to be highly control oriented; high value is placed on systematic organising, monitoring, and control systems. In such societies, there is a belief that the environment, including people, can be moulded to fit human needs. *People* are separated from *nature*. Policy decisions in such countries are made to alter nature to fulfil people's needs (e.g. genetically modified foods, bioengineering, building dams, etc).

Asian cultures with belief systems such as Confucianism, Taoism, Islam, and Buddhism, stress harmonious relations with the world. In this view, people see no real separation between people and their natural environment, and they try to live with it peacefully. People in harmony cultures are more accepting of fate and karma.

Policy decisions in these countries attempt to protect nature while meeting people's needs. Plans and projects may have challenging goals, but they will also have flexibility built in to allow for environmental changes.

Here is a story from a harmony-based culture. As you will see, people from such cultures are more accepting of 'fate'.

> *A client's organisation in Pakistan wanted to encourage their truck drivers to wear seatbelts. One of the biggest challenges they faced was from the truck drivers themselves, who responded to the idea by saying, 'We don't believe a piece of cloth is going to save our lives. If it's time for us to die, it's time for us to die' – 'Inshallah', a 'fatalistic' approach to life. To solve this problem, we used the 'Religious – Secular' dimension, and asked one of local Imams, a religious leader, to speak to the truck drivers about the importance of preserving life.*

3. Shame – Guilt

Do you feel pressure to act a certain way coming from within yourself, or do you feel pressure coming more from the society around you?

In group-oriented cultures such as China, people are motivated by **external** societal pressure. Individuals are driven by a sense of **shame**, and are expected to demonstrate an acute sense of social sensitivity towards others in their group. Misbehaviour is avoided because of the risk of adverse social consequences.

For example, when students are sent overseas to study from countries such as Korea or India, their parents will say things like, 'We're spending a lot of money sending you overseas. Make sure you study hard and do well, because your family reputation is relying on you and if you fail then it will give our family a bad name'.

In more individualistic societies such as the USA, people are motivated by **internal** pressure or **guilt**. Individuals are taught to be internally driven and to take control of their own destiny and do things of their own volition.

4. Collectivism – Individualism

Do you prefer to work alone or as part of a group? Do you do what is best for yourself or what is best for the group you belong to? Do you have only yourself to rely on or does the group take care of you? Do you expect your employer to hire you because you have the right education and work experience or because you come from the right family or social class? Do you expect to be promoted on the basis of your performance in the organisation or on the basis of your seniority?

Australians, Canadians and Americans tend to be individualists; they use personal characteristics and achievements to define self worth. Free will and self determination are important qualities. Individual welfare is valued over that of the group, and everyone is expected to look after themselves and their immediate family.

In collectivist societies, people are concerned about the impact of their behaviour on other people and are more willing to sacrifice personal interest for the attainment of collectivist interests and harmony. The will of the group determines members' beliefs and behaviour. Or as the Japanese saying goes, 'The nail that sticks out will be pounded down'. Group harmony, loyalty and unity, are emphasised. As such, tight social networks in which people strongly distinguish between their own groups and other groups characterise collectivist societies.

Here is a story that demonstrates the difference between individualistic and collectivist cultures.

*My friend Duncan is from Boston and the USA is considered to be an individualistic culture. Many years ago, our families had a picnic in the Botanical Gardens. Coming from a collectivist culture, I bought food for **everybody** to share. Duncan however, coming from an individualistic culture, bought food only for **himself** and **his** family. We laid our food out. My internal dialogue was, 'Gosh this person didn't bring any food to share! How **stingy**'. Duncan's internal dialogue, on the other hand, was 'They have brought so much food! How **wasteful**'. We were both operating from completely different cultural paradigms.*

5. Religious – Secular

Do you feel that you bring your religion or spiritual understandings with you to work? Do your religious followings and practices impact on your work life?

Some cultures believe that there has to be a separation of state from religion and would therefore promote a secular approach of development. Religion is not an important factor to be considered in one's daily work.

However, in religious cultures, such as the Middle East, we need to remain conscious that religion and work are intertwined. We need to be aware of Halal and Kosher foods, prayer times, and changing operating hours, for example, during the month of Ramadan.

6. Hierarchical – Equality

Do you show respect to your elders? If you hold a senior position in your organisation, do you expect those less experienced or younger than you to address you formally?

In hierarchical cultures, inequality is seen as normal and is accepted as part of life. Titles and class position are very important. Those in authority exercise power in an autocratic and paternalistic manner. They are assumed to have a *right* to power, either by virtue of inheritance or superior expertise. In these cultures, people feel dependent on those in authority, expect direction from them, and are cautious about disagreeing with or challenging them. They learn strict obedience as children, which usually carries over into adulthood.

Countries under prolonged, direct domination of the Roman Empire, derivative states such as the former Spanish and Portuguese colonies in the western hemisphere, and those of Confucian bureaucracy such as China, Korea, and Japan, tend to be hierarchical.

By contrast, in a more equality-based culture, value is placed on minimising levels of power, including status differences. People expect to have more *control* and expect those in authority to involve them in decision-making in a consultative or even participatory manner. Young people are treated as equals as soon as they are ready and, as adults, they usually expect to be treated in the same way by those in authority.

These societies include those with more fragmented, tribal origins such as the Germanic, Scandinavian, or Anglo countries, as well as those with more democratic, egalitarian origins like America and Australia.

Here is a story that demonstrates the difference between hierarchical and equality-based cultures.

> One of my clients, a high potential manager, was sent from Australia to Thailand on an assignment. Thailand is a 'hierarchical' culture. Coming from Australia, an equality-based culture, my client was used to calling everybody by their first names, even senior mangers. He went to Thailand and continued to do the same. He was seen to be

rude and arrogant by the Thais.

My client was treating everyone as 'equals' in an hierarchical culture, thus creating a lack of cohesion.

7. Polychronic – Monochronic time orientation

At work, do you focus on many projects at the one time, or do you like to complete one project before commencing the next?

Cultures vary on their long term or short-term time orientations. Anthropologist, Edward Hall, coined the term 'polychronic' for cultures that juggle many tasks at the same time and 'monochronic' for those that organise single tasks into linear sequences.

Monochronic people, such as Australians, like planning and keeping to plans and schedules once they are made. They typically try to do one thing at a time and take time commitments seriously. People with a polychronic view of time usually try to do several things at the same time. Time commitments are seen as desirable rather than absolute.

Most Asian cultures are polychronic, in that people change plans easily and place more value on the satisfactory completion of interactions with others.

Monochronic cultures tend to see polychronic organisations as disorganised and unreliable and their own style as organised and focused. Polychronic cultures tend to see the monochronic style as heartless, mechanical and money oriented.

Here is a story I like that illustrates the difference between monochronic and polychronic time orientation.

> *One of my friends was teaching in a university in Johannesburg. He had an appointment with his student at nine o'clock in the morning. His student turned up at five o'clock in the evening, just as he was about to leave. He said to the student, 'The appointment was for nine in the morning'. The student turned to him and said, 'Sir, it's still the same day'!*

8. High – Low context form of communication

When you say 'yes', does it always mean 'yes', or may it sometimes mean 'maybe' or 'no'? Anthropologists define cultures that depend on indirect communication as high context cultures. In these cultures, only understanding the social, political, or personal context of the situation can interpret words. They tend to rely more on **nonverbal** cues such as facial expressions or body language, and verbal skills are generally less important. What is unspoken may be just as important as the spoken word in building and maintaining relationships. High context cultures also tend to be relationship centred.

In low context cultures such as Australia, communication means that **what is said is what is meant**. That is, 'mean what you say, say what you mean'. Stress is placed on saying exactly what you mean. The best communication in these cultures, is that which contains as many facts, and as much information and detail as possible. The meaning of a message is conveyed by the words themselves. These cultures are primarily task centred.

High context is always about what's *not* said. Here is a story that illustrates the difference between high context and low context cultures.

> *A client gave a presentation in Korea, and at the end he was told, 'It was interesting, thank you, we'll give it careful consideration'. He was feeling very pleased with himself until his Korean colleague said, 'It was terrible. They didn't like it'. Her intepretation was based on the tone, manner and language with which they had delivered the feedback, compared to just the* ***words***.

9. Femininity – Masculinity

Do you believe that conflict is best solved through argument and 'fighting it out' or through negotiation and *compromise*?

In masculine oriented cultures, gender roles are clearly distinct (men are supposed to be assertive, tough and focused on material success, whereas women are supposed to be modest, tender and concerned with the quality of life). These cultures praise aggression, decisiveness and competitiveness. Conflict is settled by fighting it out (or arguing), and great value is placed on power, grandeur and achievement outside of the home. These cultures are also generally task oriented.

Masculinity has long been the dominant way of doing business, but relatively recent recognition of the value of cooperation, teamwork and sustained relationships focuses on the feminine side of business and organisation.

There are relatively few feminine cultures owing to the nearly universal, traditional gender roles of the physically dominant male taking responsibility for providing and protecting, and the child bearing and child rearing female assuming domestic responsibilities. However, in feminine cultures in some parts of Scandinavia and Latin America, gender roles tend to overlap – both men and women are supposed to be modest, tender and concerned with the quality of life. Great value is placed on caring for others, nurturing and harmony, and conflict is settled by negotiation and compromise. In a highly feminine culture, *balance* between work life and personal life is important.

Now, take a moment to fill out your own chart. Place a dot on the horizontal line based on where you see yourself on the continuum. Next, join all the nine dots vertically and observe the pattern. How varied and severe are the horizontal lines? Are your lines mostly on the left, are they on the right or are they in the middle?

My nine dimension chart – my cultural mirror

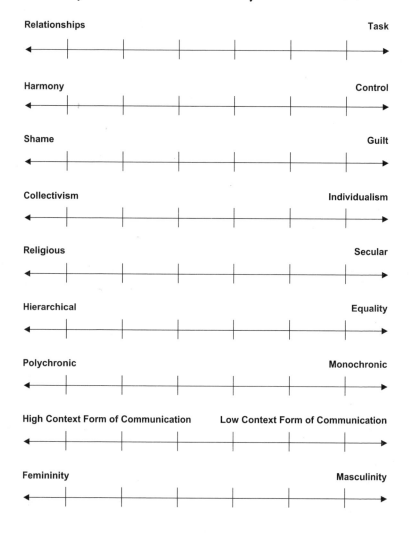

Now, consider the culture, society and norms of someone with whom you work or a neighbour who may have been raised in another country or society. Plot the characteristics, preferences and style of that person on the same chart and notice the differences.

Your sensitivity to, and awareness of, these differences is of **critical importance** in dealing with those with whom you work, live and interact. If you remember and consider these values and preferences, you will find it easier to work through obstacles and discuss and explain tasks and direction.

Remember that your culture is very familiar to you and it is the filter through which you see the world. The same holds true for those who were taught and raised in another culture. Although you may speak a common language and you are usually able to exchange words, **you are not necessarily communicating unless you consider their cultural frame**. That is the first step in understanding and taming the elephant.

People with cultural mirrors mainly on the left have more relationship, group-based cultures and values. Those who are mainly on the right are from more individualistic, task-oriented cultures.

Let's look at the charts for some specific countries. The data was supplied by participants from workshops I have facilitated around the world. Therefore you may notice discrepancies between what you perceive to be The Cultural Mirror of a particular country.

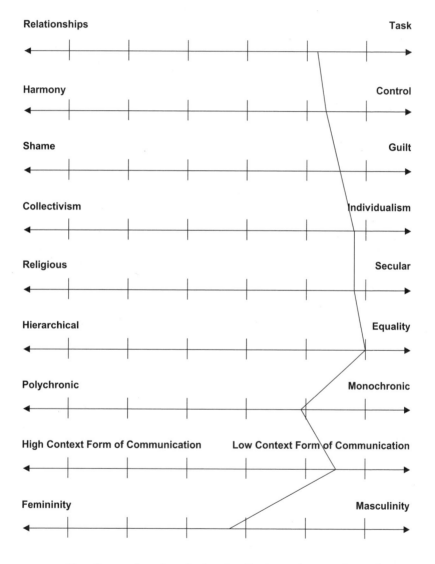

The Cultural Mirror
Culture: Australia

Equality tends to be a high value for Australians. What influence would this have on interactions?

The Cultural Mirror
Culture: China

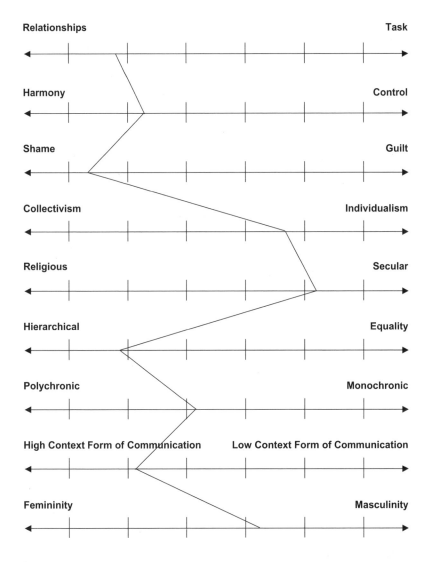

One dimension that is important for the Chinese is relationships. What influence would this have on interactions?

The Cultural Mirror
Culture: Holland

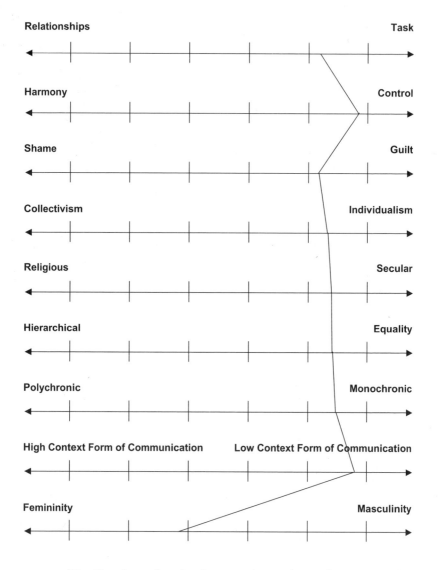

The Dutch tend to be direct and straight to the point. What influence would this have on interactions?

The Cultural Mirror
Culture: India

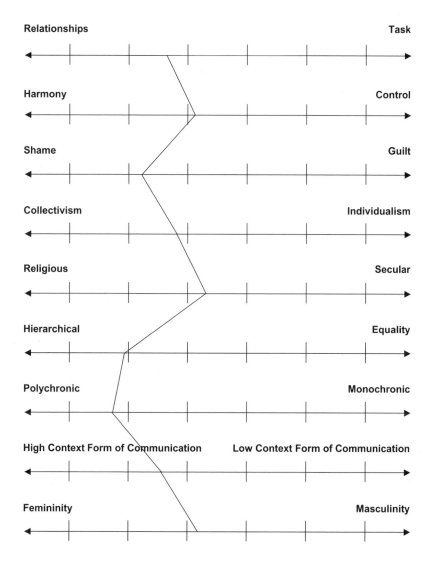

The Indians have a concept called "Indian stretch time". What influence would this have on interactions?

How would you go about forming a cohesive team of people from these different cultures?

As mentioned earlier, one of the biggest cultural gaps is that we interpret other people's behaviours through the lens of our cultural values and this is often the cause of cultural clashes. We therefore need to move from ethnocentrism to ethno-relativism. **Ethno-relativism** is the ability to look at things from different perspectives. As we constantly, but subconsciously, evaluate behaviours, we must maintain awareness that people from other cultures often behave in ways that make sense to them and not to us. See the chart below.

A developmental model of intercultural sensitivity

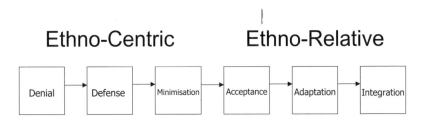

(MJ Bennett, 1986)

If you want to succeed globally, then moving to having an ethno-relative mindset is critical. In the post-modern world there are no definites – just a working towards a commonality of interests.

The better we all understand each other, the better we will do business together, create innovation and reduce conflict. We can all ride the same elephant – **with understanding.**

If we react to diversity or difference by becoming defensive, denying or minimising the differences or the appropriateness of a particular culture, we are likely to create more problems than we solve.

On the other hand, if we demonstrate acceptance and the willingness to adapt to these differences, and to integrate all group members and perspectives into the final solution, the solution will be richer and more successful for all concerned.

Let's investigate the impact of perception on culture in the next chapter.

CHAPTER 6

PERCEPTION AND INFERENCE:
HOW WE SEE THE ELEPHANT

"Actions I take are totally decided by the perceptions I have."
Edward De Bono

We now come to the part played by perception and inference in the way we relate with **other** cultures. Perception is another lens through which we see and experience the world. Perception is the process by which we select, organise and evaluate stimuli from the external environment to make it meaningful for ourselves. It is also one of the ways that determines our behaviour towards others.

Perception is neither innate nor absolute

- perception is **learned** – it is formed by our beliefs, values and experiences
- perception is **selective** – with the constant barrage of stimuli available, we screen much of it out, and only selected information passes to the conscious mind
- perception is **culturally determined and thus consistent**
- perception is **often inaccurate** – due to the many filters mentioned above our perceptions are often distorted, and even self-created. We perceive things according to what we have been trained to see, and to our cultural map.

Look at the triangles below. What do you see?

Now read each triangle carefully, **word by word**. Did you "see" the grammatical error in both the statements? If you can't, then look again.

How about the illustration below? Do you think the lines on the checkerboard are straight or crooked?

The Perception Checkerboard

When we consider perception, we must also consider inference. The following model will help you understand how we take actions based on our perceptions.

The ladder of inference is based on the work of Senge and his associates. It highlights that our mental models affect what we see, do and think.

We climb this ladder

- from observable data gleaned from experience
- to the data we select from what we observe
- to the personal and cultural meanings we add
- to the assumptions we make based on those meanings
- to the conclusions we draw based on the assumptions we make
- to the beliefs we hold about the world and the generalisations we make based on them
- to the actions we take based on those beliefs.

And this is a repeating cycle. In other words, we see what we want to see. Our perception is true for us. For example, if you have a belief that people with beards cannot be trusted, then you will find evidence to support that belief.

The ladder of inference

actions

beliefs

conclusions

assumptions

meanings

"selected" data

"observable" data

(Senge et al, 1994)

The D/I/E model

Another model useful to helping us understand how we perceive the world is the **D/I/E** model:

> **DESCRIPTION** – what happens (factual)
>
> **INTERPRETATION** – what it means (this will be coloured by our conditioning and perceptions)
>
> **EVALUATION** – how we judge it

Let's take the case of you talking to someone. If they look you in the eye – that is a fact or **description**. If you believe it conveys sincerity and honesty, that's an **interpretation**. If you believe that if they don't look you in the eye then they are probably telling you a lie, that's an **evaluation**. Apart from the "fact" or description, all else is dependent on your cultural background and perception. Before we leave the topic of perception, let us explore this issue in another way.

Here is a story I like. It is adapted from Mattock. Please read it carefully and consider the characters, motives and outcomes the story describes.

> *There is a river. Beside the river, in a little house, lives Lucy. Peter and Michael live on the other side of the river. Lucy is in love with Peter, and Michael is in love with Lucy. Lucy doesn't know what to do. She goes to her friend William and asks his opinion.*
> *"Perfectly simple", says William. "If you love Peter, go and tell him". "Okay", says Lucy.*
> *She goes to the river where she meets David, the boat man. "Please, will you take me across the river, David?" "Of course", says David. "What time do you want to return?" "I don't really know", Lucy confesses. "Why do you ask?" David explains that he has a contract*

down the river a few minutes after six o'clock, and that if Lucy wants to ride the ferry home, she must be at the landing stage before six o'clock.

They cross the river. Lucy goes to Peter's house and knocks on his door. Peter opens the door. Lucy says, "Peter, I love you". Peter cannot resist the temptation. He makes love to Lucy. When Lucy recovers from her delirium, she becomes upset at the thought that Peter has taken advantage of her.

She runs out the door and travels along the riverbank to the house where Michael lives. When Michael sees Lucy coming, he is very happy. He loves her very much and cannot wait to see her. He opens the door and sees she is clearly troubled.

Michael says, "Come in you poor girl and tell me all about it". Lucy enters Michael's home and tells him all about what has happened. Michael becomes upset and he asks Lucy to leave.

When Lucy arrives at the landing stage, it is one minute past six. David has cast off and is rowing away from the jetty. Lucy calls to him, "David, please, will you take me home?" David points to his watch. "I'm sorry Lucy. I warned you", and he rows away.

In desperation, Lucy decides to swim home. In midstream she drowns.

Peter

Lucy

Michael

David

Lucy's House

William

There are five characters in this story. Please rank these characters in order of their responsibility for Lucy's death, 1 being for most responsible and 5 for least responsible.

1. _LUCY_
2. _PETER_
3. _DAVID_
4. _MICHAEL_
5. _WILLIAM_

Why did you rank the characters in that order? Specifically consider this question as it relates to the person you thought was the most responsible for Lucy's death and the person you held least accountable.

If you are from a Western culture, it is likely that you said that Lucy was the most responsible for her own death. William is usually considered the least responsible.

Are there cultures in the world that would hold William the most responsible for Lucy's death? What sort of cultures? Those that frown on putting a person in a vulnerable situation, without showing them the consequences of their actions. These are cultures where the giving of advice is taken seriously. In other words, cultures that value wisdom would hold William responsible because he gave the advice.

You can see then that the things we hold dear will affect how we look at decisions. We use our own core values and perceptions to make sense of a situation. We tend to get a little bit of information and we fill in the blanks. This is due to cognitive consistency – making sense of the world.

What impact does this have?

It is very difficult to make non-evaluative judgments because perception and inference are complex and subjective. We constantly evaluate others, based on our own cultural norms and values, and this can be problematic when working across cultures.

How many faces do you see here?

How about here?

Look carefully and consider the dark spaces in the pictures. There are actually a number of faces in these pictures, and you can see them quite well when you look for them.

Culture and communication are really about our perceptions – what we *think* we see and what we are *prepared* to see. And what we actually do see.

Now that we understand how much our perceptions are affected by our conditioning and culture, we are in a better position to acknowledge and understand cultural diversity. Let's look at how to manage it in the next chapter.

CHAPTER 7

MANAGING CULTURAL DIVERSITY AND DIFFERENCE: HOW TO CLIMB ON THE ELEPHANT

"It's hard to think outside the square when you are in it."
Handy, 2002

As we have seen, the first step to managing cultural diversity is to understand it. The second is to respect the differences between cultures, and to celebrate how each culture can enrich us. The model below was adapted from Adler. Look at the descriptors on both the vertical axis and horizontal axis and reflect on the suggested solutions.

Consider the differences in conflict management styles from each dimension of the graph above. There are benefits and costs to each style.

Cultural dominance

- positions are win/lose
- the positions may be aggressive and uncooperative
- the individual pursues their own concerns at the other's expense
- individuals operate in a power-oriented mode.

This approach has historically been used by organisations that had considerably more power than their counterparts – for example, because they were larger, more technologically advanced or more financially successful.

Benefits: sense of power
Costs: alienating behaviour, stressful, invites aggression.
The historical inevitability of the roles eventually being reversed.

Cultural avoidance

- positions are lose/lose
- the individual does not pursue their own concerns or those of the other person
- the individual does not address, but in fact avoids conflict.

Cultural avoidance is to act as if there are no differences – to act as if no conflict exists. Asian leaders use this approach most frequently and it often emphasises "saving face" over openly and explicitly confronting all the details and conflict inherent in a particular situation.

Cultural avoidance is most commonly used when the unresolved issue is less important than the overall relationship or contract.

Benefits: Creates a sense of safety, space, security.
Costs: Alienating, stressful, invites aggression.

Cultural accommodation

- position is lose/win
- the individual is willing to lose to "keep the peace"
- individuals are unassertive, yet cooperative
- individuals let go of their concerns out of consideration for the other person
- soothing, passive, self-sacrificing.

Individuals who learn the local language of countries in which they work are using a cultural accommodation strategy.

For example, an Australian businessperson used cultural accommodation in Japan when attempting to get a first contract from a particularly important potential Japanese buyer.

The Australian spent the first two weeks in Kobe and Osaka dining and playing golf with the Japanese counterpart without scheduling any formal meetings on the product. While his Australian boss in Melbourne believed his colleague had confused his business trip with a vacation, the Australian business man adapted perfectly to the Japanese style of doing business, and allowed the Japanese to get to know him and build a relationship with him before he focused on the details of the contract and the task. Needless to say, the Australian got the contract.

Benefits: Friendship and "peace".
Costs: The individual may get "used"; losing self-respect and respect from others; stressful; individual needs are often sacrificed.

Cultural compromise

- position is 'half win/half win' or 'half lose/half lose'
- this creates a 50% solution
- it is an intermediate approach between assertion and cooperation
- the approach aims to find expedient, quick solutions
- the individual splits the difference, and exchanges concessions
- this is a middle-ground position.

Using cultural compromise implies that both sides will concede something in order to work more successfully with one another. When Malaysian and Thai potential joint venture partners held initial meetings, they alternated between Kuala Lumpur and Bangkok so that each side had to travel to only half the meetings. Using that approach, neither side endured the inconvenience of 100% of the travel and time away from their own headquarters.

In compromised situations, the more powerful partner often gives up less than the less powerful partner. However, both sides make concessions for the business relationship to succeed.

Benefits: A quicker solution is often achieved.

Costs: Solutions are not necessarily the best, nor long lasting, and all the needs of both parties are not satisfied.

Cultural Synergy

- position is "win/win"
- the individual wants a solution that meets the needs of **both** parties
- the position is both assertive and cooperative
- individuals work in a **problem-solving** mode

- the approach requires a detailed analysis of an issue, to identify the underlying concerns of all parties and individuals and to find a solution that satisfies both sets of goals
- the parties explore **creative solutions.**

This approach of cultural synergy develops new solutions to problems with respect to each of the underlying cultures. Leaders first define problems from the perspectives of **all** cultures involved. They then analyse the patterns that make each cultural behaviour logical from its own perspective, and create solutions that foster organisational effectiveness and productivity without violating the norms of any of the cultures involved.

This approach creates organisational solutions to problems by using cultural diversity as **a resource** and an advantage to the organisation.

Although the most time consuming and the one requiring a major commitment of all involved parties, this is the approach that will lead to the most harmonious solutions and is the most likely to produce long term, sustainable and profitable joint ventures. This approach truly gives us the smoothest elephant ride.

> **Benefits**: High self-esteem; empowering; the needs of all parties are respected; relationships are protected and enhanced.
>
> **Costs**: Requires time, effort, commitment, and the willingness to have an effective long-term resolution.

(These models were adapted from Adler, 1997)

Reflect on your preference when dealing with conflict. What is your cultural norm? How can you achieve cultural synergy from conflict? Let's look at that in the next chapter.

CHAPTER 8

USING CULTURAL INTELLIGENCE:
THE ELEPHANT SITS AT THE TABLE

"Let us give up the fighting mind and develop the dancing spirit, so that our timing and our actions become in tune with each situation."
F.F. Crum

All business transactions are between people and therefore require communication.

Effective communicators are aware of the lens through which they view the world.

Effective cross-cultural communicators are aware of the **many lenses** that affect their view and how these impact on others. They are also aware of the many lenses that affect the others' view and how this could impact on interaction.

They constantly attempt to be open and non-judgmental.

Look at the model on the following page. It provides a way to approach problem-solving options.

Cultural mindfulness

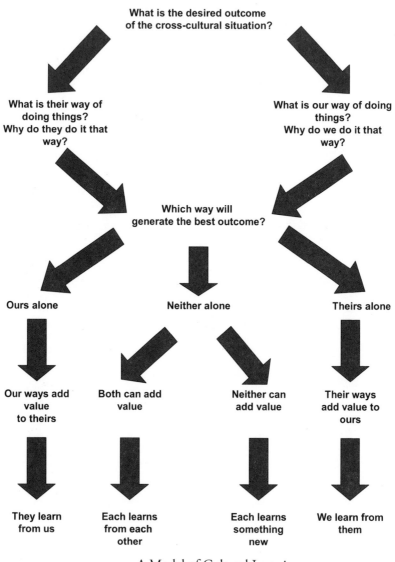

A Model of Cultural Learning
(Hoecklin 1995)

All effective communication begins with a conscious attitude and mindfulness; a genuine desire to understand and to make oneself understood. It is imperative that you take responsibility for understanding and being understood. Mindfulness is a skill. It is a mindset that requires practise. It requires you to suspend judgment, be aware that you come from a culture and it is different to, but no better or worse than, any other. It requires the awareness that cross-cultural communication is a continuous learning and relearning process. It requires genuineness. Being more mindful of cultural diversity, and of your own impact on the outcome of cross-cultural interaction, will improve your behavioural skills, enhance your knowledge, and make you even more mindful.

If you review and embrace the following information, you will find it easier to remain mindful of cultural and language differences and to accommodate those differences.

Do	Do NOT
Analyse the identity and background of the person with whom you will be working: • *What is their title and position? What do you know about their culture, customs, language, and country?* • *What is their language proficiency?* • *What is their interest in, and knowledge of, your subject?* • *What is their attitude toward your point of view?* • *What motivates them?*	Shout as though your associates were deaf, or speak too fast. The major complaint of non-native English individuals is that most English people talk too fast.

Do	Do NOT
Be prepared with information about your country, since your associates may be interested to know facts and information about you as well.	Use slang or terms borrowed from sports or other cultural context, e.g. 'struck out', 'can't get to first base', 'run a tight ship', 'catch-22'.
Respect your associates' effort and willingness to communicate in your language.	Speak so slowly that you are insulting or patronising, use jargon, idiomatic phrases, colloquialisms or acronyms, or speak in complicated sentences.
Use a slow, steady speaking pace; speak clearly, comprehensibly and precisely.	Change topics abruptly.
Keep your language simple. Many words have multiple meanings, and non-native speakers are more likely to know the first or second most common meanings.	Use 'word pictures' – constructs that depend on invoking a particular mental image, e.g. 'run that by me', 'slice of the pie'.
Conform to basic grammar rules more strictly than is common in everyday conversation. Make sure that sentences express a complete thought.	Pronounce words imprecisely, swallow words, ramble, mumble, digress aimlessly or use long anecdotes.
Be friendly and respectful.	Point at an individual (if necessary, use the fully spread hand or closed fist to point).
Smile and laugh *with* your friends and associates – not *at* them!	Use jokes – often they are irrelevant, sometimes they are offensive, and they are usually culture bound.

Do	Do NOT
Be open-minded and flexible.	Judge or analyse others from your own cultural perspective.
Give your friends and associates time to process and understand what you are saying.	Assume that someone understands what you are saying because they do not respond.
Listen actively and test for understanding, and encourage your cross-cultural friends to do the same.	Become short-tempered or impatient if someone wishes to build a relationship with you before they get down to business.
Notice non-verbal communication – watch people's eyes, face and gestures to pick up non-verbal cues.	Underestimate the importance of non-verbal communication – how you hold yourself, move, dress, use your hands, look at people, your inflection and facial expressions are all important.
Be aware of when 'yes' may mean something other than 'yes'.	Use redundancy and unnecessary quantification, as they are confusing to the non-native speaker.
Use written communication carefully, checking for spelling of names, punctuation and meaning. Modify your spelling of words, if required, e.g. (colour versus color, cheque versus check).	Say something in a vague way. Explain your point with examples and use more than one way to make your point so that you will be understood.

Do	Do NOT
Ask yourself if you have: • done everything you should do • made the right impression • worked in synergy with the person or group • made your cross-cultural friends and associates feel comfortable.	Ignore what others think or how they behave or discount their opinions as unimportant because you do not understand them.

If you can remain mindful of these important techniques and methods of cross-cultural communication, you are much more likely to understand and to be understood.

Cultural intelligence (CQ)

"In approaching cross-cultural situations, effective business people...assume difference until similarity is proven. They recognise that all behaviour makes sense through the eyes of the person behaving and that logic and rationale are culturally relative. In cross-cultural business situations, labeling behaviour as bizarre usually reflects culturally based misperception, misinterpretation, and misevaluation..."

(Adler 1997)

What is Cultural Intelligence? As mentioned in Chapter One, Cultural Intelligence is the combination of cultural awareness, knowledge, cultural mindfulness and behavioural skills.

It is depicted in the following illustration.

Components of cultural intelligence

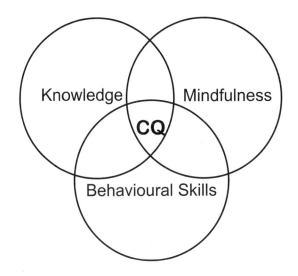

(Thomas & Inkson 2004)

As the early explorers discovered new lands, the culturally intelligent individual explores new ways to enhance the available knowledge. Transcending cultural boundaries. They seek to expand the understanding that can help their corporation become truly post-modern, global and culturally embracing.

What strategies do you think would be useful in helping you work more effectively with those whose cultural boundaries are foreign to you?

Let us look at a few of the dimensions we have already discussed in the Cultural Mirror section of this book.

Relationship Versus Task

Assume you come from a task-oriented culture. What could you do when working with people from a relationship based culture?

Spend some time building a relationship. Invest in small talk to make the person feel more comfortable. Ask friendly, but non-intrusive questions about their interests or work. When having morning tea, make it more of a social gathering. Assign a mentor. Allow time for questions.

What if you are from a relationship culture and working more with task-oriented cultures? What are a few things you could do?

Begin with an end in mind. Set the goal. Find out how you can reach your goal together. Build the relationship through the task. Give clear instructions. Ensure that meetings are short and concises. Provide procedures and manuals.

Harmony Verses Control

If you are from a control-based culture, what could do when working with people from a harmony culture?

Be mindful that open conflict is likely to be avoided.

If you are from a harmony culture, what could you do when working with people from a control-based culture?

Be aware that rigorous debate may be encouraged.

Shame Verses Guilt

When coming from a guilt-based culture, what are some of the things you could do when working with people from a shame-based culture?

Encourage participation through group based tasks to remove attention from individuals which may cause 'loss of face'.

When coming from a shame-based culture, what are some of the things you could do when working with a guilt-based culture?

Allow time for experimentation and brain storming of ideas.

Collectivism Versus Individualism

When coming from an individualistic culture, what could you do when working with people from a collectivist culture?

Break into smaller groups to increase input from individuals; give them strategies, and, if necessary, provide workshops on how to build self confidence.

When coming from a collectivist culture, what could you do when working with people from an individualistic culture?

Assign specific tasks and roles to individuals within groups – when working in a team, get each person to do individual work and bring it back to the team; reward individuals who perform well for their team's goals.

Religious Versus Secular

When coming from with a secular culture, what could you do when working with people from a religious culture?

Recognise and acknowledge; ensure breaks are given for prayer times where appropriate.

When coming from a religious culture, what could you do when working with people from a secular culture?

Acknowledge and appreciate that there are different religious and belief systems around the world.

Hierarchy Versus Equality

If you are from a hierarchical culture, what are some things you could do to work more effectively with those from an equality-based culture?

Don't act arrogantly. Show that you are willing to give and receive feedback regardless of the ranking of people in the organisation.

What if you are from an equality-based culture and working in an hierarchical-based culture?

Start by showing some respect to seniors and titles. Be conscious of names, dress codes and formalities.

Polychronic Versus Monochronic

When coming from a monochronic culture, what could you do when dealing with people from a polychronic culture?

Ensure flexibility; make sure things are prioritised; be fluid with timelines.

When coming from a polychronic culture, what could you do when dealing with people from a monochronic culture?

Be punctual, set deadlines and deliver on them. Be focussed.

High Context Versus Low Context

When coming from a low context culture, what could you do when working with a high context culture?

Be patient; be a good listener; develop good analytical skills; learn how to give circular feedback. Use analogies and metaphors.

When coming from a high context culture, what could you do when working with a low context culture?

Learn how to be direct and straightforward. Ask questions. Tell it as it is.

Femininity Versus Masculinity

When coming from a masculine culture, what could you do when working with a feminine culture?

Make sure you listen; avoid being over-aggressive; be willing to compromise.

When coming from a feminine culture, what could you do when working with people from a masculine culture?

'Keep your cool'- don't get emotional; don't be intimidated; keep your arguments concise and rational.

If you are interested in building your cultural-intelligence, review all of the dimensions on the cultural mirror, and think about how to develop your own set of recommendations to handle the cultural norms of the people with whom you most commonly interact, live and work. Ask those who come from other cultures to help with this task.

Broaden your cultural knowledge. If you are working with people from different countries, develop an understanding of their individual cultures. This will significantly improve your ability to work with each of the people on your team. **Embrace the differences**. Celebrate your own and each others' differences.

Create commonalities. Your differences can be one of the commonalities.

Constantly assess the situation. Be aware of the **D/I/E** model and ask, "Am I reading this situation correctly?" Check your assumptions by asking someone from the other culture.

Talk about culture. Have open conversations about it. Ask questions. Be curious, but courteous.

Enhance your communication skills. How do you engage people across cultures? How do you build rapport? How do you engage in small talk? How do you build relationships? How do you ask questions? How do you provide information? How do you provide feedback?

Be less judgmental about how people react to you and your culture, or to the solutions you recommend.

Become adept at conflict resolution. How do you deal with differences and disagreement? Are there ways you can do that and still maintain good relationships?

The 7 characteristics of cultural intelligence

- understanding of self
- understanding of others
- openness
- humility
- curiosity
- hardiness
- genuineness.

Gaining Cultural Intelligence – a model

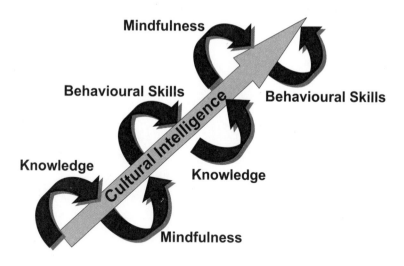

(Cultural Intelligence, D.C. Thomas & K. Inkson)

If you look at cultural intelligence as a continuous learning experience, refine your knowledge and skills every day by asking questions of yourself and others, and remain open to feedback and suggestions, you will become a role model for managing cultural diversity.

CHAPTER 9

CONCLUSION: THE ELEPHANT AND THE ROOM BECOME ONE

"If you see God within every man and woman, then you can never do harm to any man or woman."
The Bhagavad Gita

Communication is at the heart of all organisational, political and community operations and relations. It is the single most important tool we have to get things done, and to get along!

Every day, we communicate with others and whether we know it or not, our actions, our gestures, our facial expressions and our inflections mean just as much as the words we use.

Yet, the subtle and blatant differences between our cultures and societies offer plenty of opportunity for misinterpretation, as communication is manifest through symbols that differ globally in their meaning according to time, place, culture and person.

Communicating across cultures therefore becomes quite challenging when one considers that there are approximately 3000 different languages, each representing a different perceptual world.

Many nations share an official language, such as English, but even when there is a common language with which to communicate, there are many versions of that language.

Consider Australian, British and American English. In India, the official language is Hindi, but English is a "link" language among India's fifteen major languages and numerous dialects.

Although all of these people and cultures may speak the English language, the subtleties of inflection, slang and language, leave gaps that may still create obstacles in communication.

Remember that differences in attitudes and values exist in all cultures, and these differences ultimately influence communication.

This book has attempted to help you recognise the invisible elephant when communicating across cultures. It has given you a number of tools to help you understand and expand your cultural awareness and knowledge.

The world will only become smaller, and the individuals and businesses that embrace **cultural intelligence** are the ones that will prosper.

The modern world is now gone. The new, post-modern, globalised economy is with us. You might as well embrace the elephant and enjoy the ride.

Finally...

'Living' Cultural Diversity

C onsider prejudices you may have.

U se 'the platinum rule'.*

L isten attentively.

T alk with and learn from others.

U nderstand with an open mind.

R espect diversity to create synergy.

A ct in a culturally sensitive manner.

L ead with respect.

D emonstrate self awareness.

I nquire about other cultures.

V ive la différence.

E ducate yourself.

R ole model appropriate behaviour.

S eek first to understand.

I nstigate diversity practices.

T hink the talk. Walk the talk. Talk the talk.

Y ou make the difference!

* 'Treat others as they would like to be treated'.

REFERENCES

Abdullah, A. (1992). *Understanding the Malaysian Workforce. Guidelines for Managers.* Malaysian Institute of Management, Kuala Lumpur.

Abdullah, A. (1996). *Going Global. Cultural Dimensions in Malaysian Management.* Malaysian Institute of Management, Kuala Lumpur.

Adler, N. J. (1997). *International Dimensions of Organisational Behaviour.* South-Western College Publishing, Cincinnati, Ohio.

Brake, T. (2002). *Managing Globally.* Dorling Kindersley Limited, London.

Brake, T., Medina Walker, D. & Walker, T. (1995). *Doing Business Internationally. The Guide to Cross-Cultural Success.* Irwin, Illinois, New York.

Chaney, L. H. & Martin, J.S. (2000). *Intercultural Business Communication.* Prentice Hall, New Jersey.

Chu, Chin-Ning (1995). *The Asian Mind Game. A Westerner's Survival Manual.* Stealth Production, Australia.

Clawson, J. G. (1999). *Level Three Leadership. Getting Below the Surface.* Prentice Hall, Upper Saddle River, New Jersey.

Cox Jr., T. (2001). *Creating the Multicultural Organisation. A Strategy for Capturing the Power of Diversity.* Jossey-Bass Publishers, San Francisco.

Dayao, D. (2000). *Asian Business Wisdom. Lessons from the Region's Best and Brightest Business Leaders.* John Wiley and Sons, Singapore.

Duarte, D. L. & Tennant Snyder, N. (2001). *Mastering Virtual Teams. Strategies, Tools, and Techniques That Succeed* (2nd ed). Jossey-Bass Publishers, San Francisco.

Earley, P. C. & Gibson, C. B., *Multinational Work Teams. A New Perspective.* Lawrence Erlbaum Associates, New Jersey.

Elashmawi, F. & Harris, P. R. (1994). *Multi Cultural Management. New Skills for Global Success.* S. Abdul Majeed & Co, Kuala Lumpur.

Esty, K., Griffin, R. & Hirsch, M. S. (1995). *Workplace Diversity. A Manager's Guide to Solving Problems and Turning Diversity into a Competitive Advantage.* Adams Media Corporation, Massachusetts.

Fisher, G. (1998). *The Mindsets Factor in Ethnic Conflict. A Cross-Cultural Agenda.* Intercultural Press Inc., Yarmouth.

Funakawa, A. (1997). *Transcultural Management. A New Approach For Global Organisations.* Jossey-Bass Publishers, San Francisco.

Gardenswartz, L., Rowe, A., Digh, P. & Bennett, M.F. (2003). The Global Diversity Desk Reference: Managing an International Workforce. Pfeiffer Publishing, San Francisco, US.

Ghoshal, S. & Bartlett, C. A. (1998). *Managing Across Borders. The Transnational Solution.* Random House Business Books, London.

Goleman, D. (1996). *Emotional Intelligence. Why It Can Matter More Than IQ.* Bloomsbury, London.

Goldsmith, M., Greenberg, C., Robertson, A. & Hu-Chan, M. (2003). *Global Leadership – The Next Generation.* Financial Times Prentice Hall, New Jersey.

Handy,C (2002) *The Elephant and the Flea ,* Arrow, The Random House Group, London

Harris, P. R. & Moran, R. T. (2000). *Managing Cultural Strategies. Leadership Strategies for a New World of Business.* Gulf Publishing Company, Houston, Texas.

Hesselbein, F., Goldsmith, M. & Beckhard, R. (eds). (1996). *The Leader of the Future. New Visions, Strategies, and Practices for the Next Era.* Jossey-Bass Publishers, San Francisco.

Hoecklin, L. (1995). *Managing Cultural Differences. Strategies for Competitive Advantage.* Addison-Wesley, Workingham, England.

Hofstede, G. (1994). *Cultures and Organisations.* Harper Collins Publishers, London

Hofstede, G. (1980). *Culture's Consequences.* Sage Publications, Beverley Hills, USA.

Holden, N. J. (2002). *Cross-Cultural Management. A Knowledge Management Perspective.* Financial Times Prentice Hall, Harlow, Essex.

Irwin, H. (1996). *Communicating with Asia. Understanding People and Customs.* Allen & Unwin, St. Leonards, NSW.

James, D. L. (1995). *The executive guide to Asia-Pacific Communications. Doing business throughout Asia and the Pacific.* Allen & Unwin, St. Leonards, NSW.

Jackson, P. (ed). (1999). *Virtual Working. Social and organisational dynamics.* Routledge, London & New York.

Kwang, N. A. (2001). Why Asians Are Less Creative than Westerners. Prentice Hall, Singapore.

LeBaron, M. (2003). *Bridging Cultural Conflicts. A New Approach for a Changing World.* Jossey-Bass, San Francisco.

Leung, K. & Tjosvold D. (1998). *Conflict Management in the Asia Pacific. Assumptions and Approaches in Diverse Cultures.* John Wiley & Sons, Singapore.

Lewis, R. D. (2003). *The Cultural Imperative. Global Trends in the 21st Century.* Intercultural Press, Maine.

Mark, E. (1999). *Breaking Through Culture Shock. What You Need to Succeed in International Business.* Nicholas Brealey Publishing, London.

Mattock, J (1991). *International Management: An Essential Guide to Cross Cultural Business.* Kogan Page, London.

Mole, J. (1995). *Mind Your Manners. Managing Business Cultures in Europe.* Nicholas Brealey Publishing, London.

Morrison, T., Conaway, W. A. & Borden, G. A. (1994). *Kiss, Bow, or Shake Hands. How to Do Business in Sixty Countries.* Adams Media Corporation, Holbrook, Massachusetts.

Rhinesmith, S. H. (1996). *A Manager's Guide to Globalisation. Six Skills for Success in a Changing World.* Mc-Graw Hill, New York.

Rosen, R., Digh, P., Singer, M. & Phillips, C (2000). *Lessons on Business Leadership and National Cultures.* Simon & Schuster, New York.

Rosinski, P. (2003). *Coaching Across Cultures.* Nicholas Brealey Publishing, London.

Sabath, A. (1999). *International Business Etiquette. Asia & The Pacific Rim.* Career Press, Franklin Lakes, New Jersey.

Schneider, S. C. & Barsoux, J-L. (1997). *Managing Across Cultures.* Financial Times Prentice Hall, Essex.

Seelye, H. N & Seelye-James, A. (1995). *Culture Clash. Managing in a Multicultural World.* NTC Business Books, Illinois.

Shtogren, J. A. (ed). (1999). *Skyhooks for Leadership. A New Framework That Brings Together Five Decades of Thought – From Maslow to Senge.* Amacom, New York.

Simmons, M., 1996, *New Leadership for Women and Men: Building an Inclusive Organisation*, Gower Publishing Limited, Hampshire, UK

Singer, M. R. (1998). *Perception and Identity in Intercultural Communication.* Intercultural Press Inc., Yarmouth.

Storti, C. (1990). *The Art of Crossing Cultures.* Intercultural Press, Inc., Yarmouth, Maine.

Thomas, D.C., & Inkson, K. (2004). *Cultural Intelligence: People Skills for Global Business.* Berrett-Koehler, San Francisco.

Trompenaars, F. & Hampden-Turner, C. (2000). *Building Cross-Cultural Competence.* Chicester, UK: John Wiley & Sons, Ltd.

Trompenaars, F. & Hampden-Turner, C. (1997). *Mastering the Infinite Game: How East Asian Values are Transforming Business Practices.* Oxford, UK: Capstone Publishing Ltd.

Trompenaars, F. (1993). *Riding the Waves of Culture. Understanding Cultural Diversity in Business.* London: Nicholas Brealey Publishing Ltd.

Yip, G. S. (2000). *Asian Advantage. Key Strategies for Winning in the Asia-Pacific Region.* Perseus Books, Cambridge, Massachusetts.

APPENDIX

Here are the Cultural Mirrors from a selection of countries. Look at them and reflect on how it influences the behaviour of people from these countries and what you would need to consider when interacting with them.

There are also two blank Cultural Mirrors for your use.

The Cultural Mirror
Culture: Venezuela

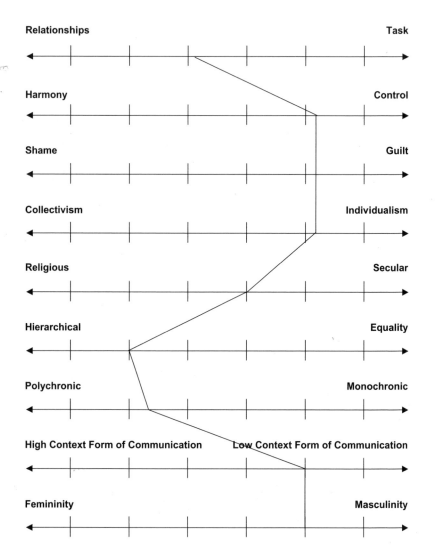

The Cultural Mirror
Culture: England

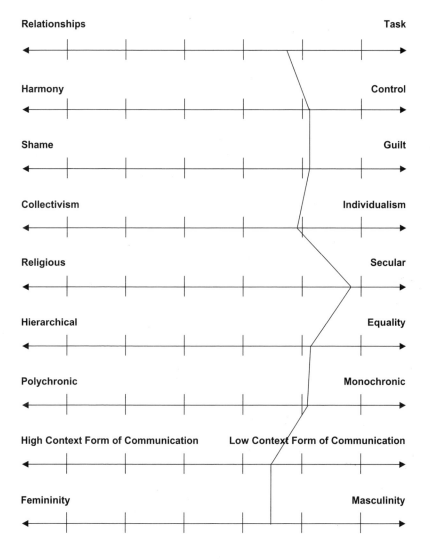

The Cultural Mirror
Culture: Kenya

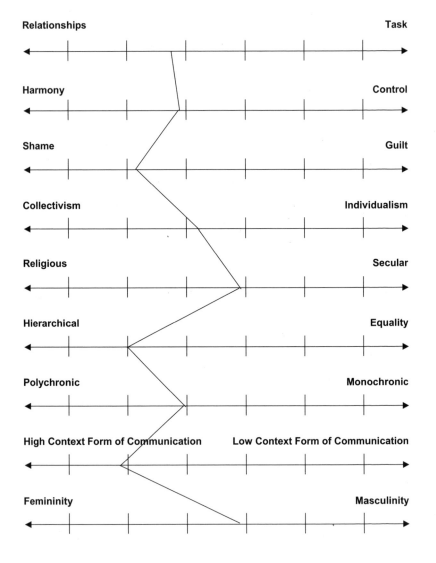

The Cultural Mirror
Culture: Japan

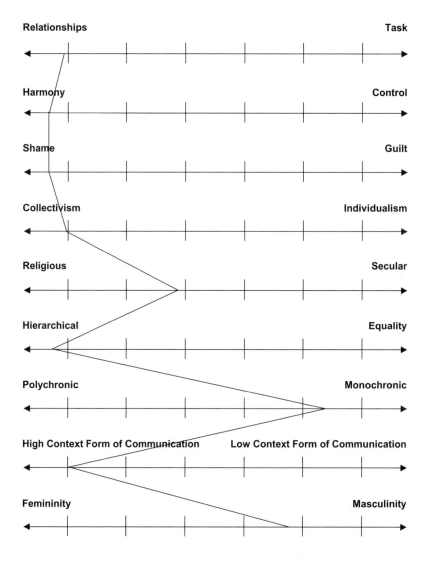

The Cultural Mirror
Culture: Oman

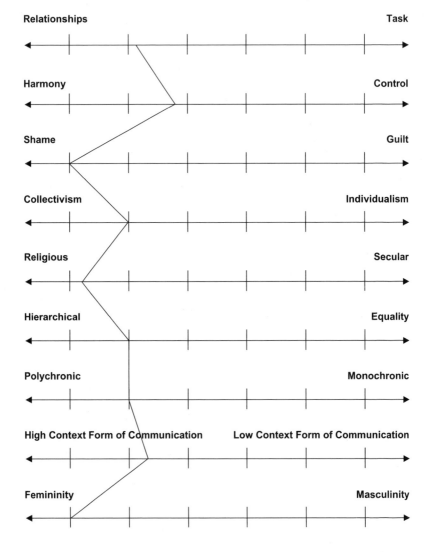

The Cultural Mirror
Culture: Singapore

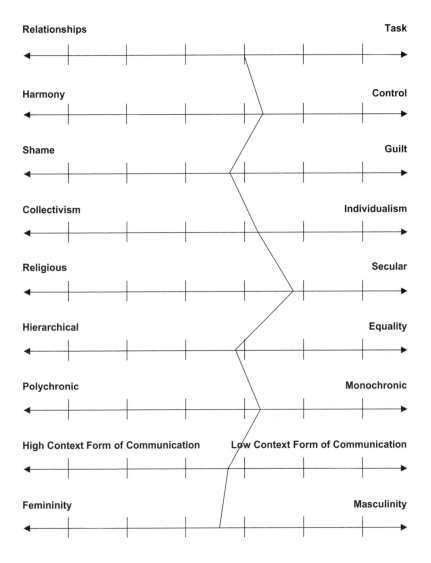

The Cultural Mirror
Culture: USA

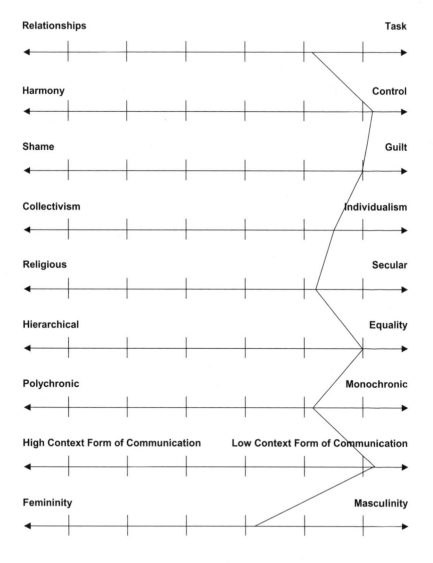

The Cultural Mirror
Culture: Germany

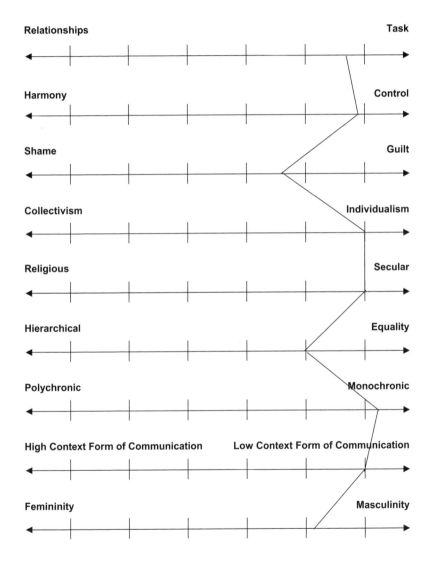

The Cultural Mirror

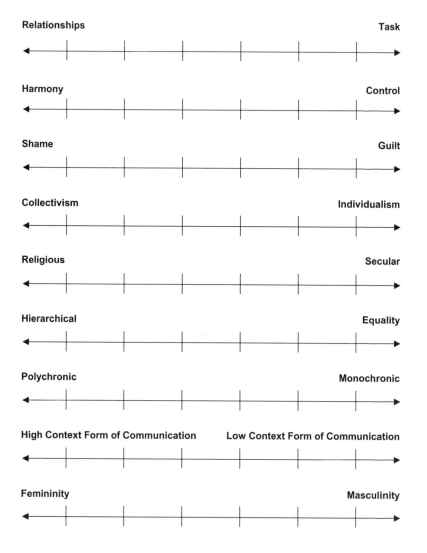

The Cultural Mirror

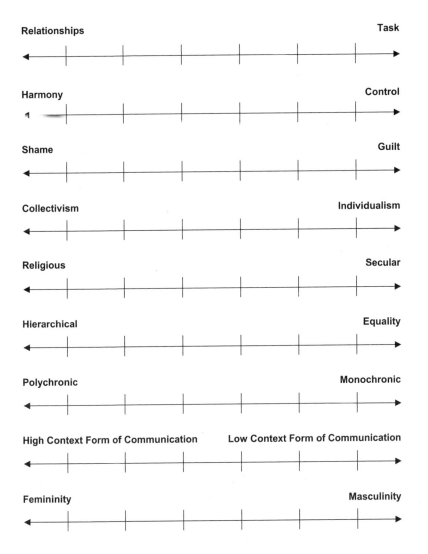

Relationships — Task

Harmony — Control

Shame — Guilt

Collectivism — Individualism

Religious — Secular

Hierarchical — Equality

Polychronic — Monochronic

High Context Form of Communication — Low Context Form of Communication

Femininity — Masculinity

Notes

Notes

cultural synergies

INTERCULTURAL MANAGEMENT CONSULTANTS

About Cultural Synergies

Established in 1992, Cultural Synergies is a leading intercultural and diversity consultancy dedicated to working collaboratively with individuals and organisations to improve effectiveness in the global marketplace. We provide value-based consultation, research, education, training and coaching around the world.

We have successfully completed projects globally for prestigious clients such as Royal Dutch Shell, AXA, Toyota, Ingersoll-Rand, Cochlear, AchieveGlobal, Rohm & Haas, Exxon-Mobil Oil, Autoliv, Mount Eliza Business School, The University of Melbourne, Hewlett Packard, Bendigo Bank, British Petroleum and ANZ Bank.

Services include:

Diversity and Inclusion
- Managing and leading workforce diversity and inclusion
- Strategic planning for diversity and inclusion
- Gender, generational and work/life balance workshops

Team-building
- Working effectively in virtual teams
- Working successfully in multicultural teams

Cultural Expertise
- Leadership across culture, distance and time
- Negotiating across cultures
- Customer service across cultures
- Selling and marketing across cultures

When organisations work with Cultural Synergies they get the experience and expertise of a network of professionals who are diverse, innovative, results oriented, and committed to making a difference. All our products and services are customised to meet the specific requirements of our clients.

For more information about our services, please contact us at:

Cultural Synergies Pty Ltd
Level 5, Causeway House
306 Little Collins Street
Melbourne VIC 3000
Australia
Tel: +61 3 9654 6161
Fax: +61 3 9650 7350
Web: www.culturalsynergies.com

About Tom Verghese

Tom Verghese lives and breathes cultural diversity. Of Indian origin, born and raised in multi-ethnic Malaysia, he now lives in Australia with his English-born wife, Alison, children, Jemma and Rajesh, and pets, Holly and Posie. A passionate teacher, traveller, father, student, linguist and philosopher, he brings a broad perspective of East and West to life.

Tom holds a degree in management, as well as a Graduate Diploma and Masters in Education and Training. His qualifications, experience and multicultural skills position him as a leading international presenter in the areas of cultural diversity and cross-cultural leadership. During his more than 15 years of consulting, he has dealt with a diverse range of people from different cultures all around the world. He is the founder and director of the consulting firm Cultural Synergies.

Known as 'The Cultural Synergist', Tom is a dynamic, enthusiastic, passionate, energetic and entertaining speaker. He is also the co-author of 'The Pillars of Growth - The Keys to Getting Exponential Growth in Your Business Today.' Tom can be contacted at:

Cultural Synergies Pty Ltd
Level 5, Causeway House
306 Little Collins Street
Melbourne VIC 3000
Australia
Tel: +61 3 9654 6161
Fax: +61 3 9650 7350
Email: tom.verghese@culturalsynergies.com